Michael Farrell | Cocky's Joy

New Poems

GIRAMONDO POETS

Michael Farrell | Cocky's Joy

First Published 2015
from the Writing & Society Research Centre
at the University of Western Sydney
by the Giramondo Publishing Company
PO Box 752 Artarmon NSW 1570 Australia
www.giramondopublishing.com

Designed by Harry Williamson
Typeset by Andrew Davies
In 10/16pt Baskerville

Printed and bound by Ligare Book Printers
Distributed in Australia by NewSouth Books

National Library of Australia
Cataloguing-in-Publication data:

Farrell, Michael
Cocky's Joy / Michael Farrell
ISBN 978-1-922146-76-2 (pbk.)
A821.3

Acknowledgements

Award Winning Australian Writing 2013; Best Australian Poems 2011; Best Australian Poems 2012; Critical Animalia; Newcastle Poetry Prize Anthology 2011; Outcrop: Radical Australian Poetry of Land; Small Wonder: An Anthology of Prose Poems and Microfiction; Strange Stars: Queer Lights in International Poetry; The Turnrow Anthology of Australian Poetry (US); *Antipodes* (US); *Australian Book Review; Australian Poetry Journal; Blackbox Manifold* (UK); *Blue and Yellow Dog* (US); *cordite; ETZ; Four W; Higher Arc; Idiot* (Slovenia); *Lana Turner* (US); *Mascara; otoliths; Overland; Polari; rabbit; Shampoo* (US); *Shearsman* (UK); *Southerly; The Age; Upstairs at Duroc* (France); *VLAK* (Czech Republic); *Warwick Review* (UK); *Yellow Field* (US).

contents

breakfasts

two anchovies; a bowl of milk; fried crumpet

a plum; a gun; chocolate muesli

three carpet buns with jam; tuna pickle; minties

space-ground coffee; eel segments; anzac biscuits

blendered corn; blendered tofu; happy juice

toasted garlic; roasted marshmallows; insipid tea

a hundred year old cream; fresh marzipan; banknotes

whitlamian croissant; cheese a la keating; water-by-hawke

roast lamb; rice bubbles; dropped yoghurt

grated apple with curds and ghee; ginger; fruit crusts

wheaties; banana syrup; wanderlust

photo stack; recycled margarine; caramel lovecake

damper; tomato skins; mouldy honey

hammer; blue sky; homemade anti-depressants

charcoal; peanuts; cup of kikuyu dew

ricepaper scrolls; dates; stringybark garnish

celery; rosemary marmalade; pipesmoke

blessed lemonade; genuflection; knuckle rap

sunshine; bullying; ricotta

sushi; mistletoe; sighting of a pheasant

crepe soldiers; pea smoothie; twice-boiled egg

bread with icecream and shredded mint; marigolds; salt

white noise; camembert; jatz

bodysurfing; woman's day; junket

assorted fudge; icecubes; underarm baguette

mango vinegar; orange plastic; pinecone etc.

Making Love (To A Man)

Didn't think I'd hear from that man again, but there was a message in my inbox. Within five hours we were in his bedroom. His hair is not computer hair, it's straight and black: turntable hair, old school, calligraphy brush hair. He's three-dimensional: changes as I move around him, first on my feet, then on my knees. I'm on my knees – he's on his back. The bed's hard but I don't say anything. Talk only leads to more talk, well it shears off the strangeness, which has crept back since last time.

It's Melbourne so we still haven't completely undressed. Then as if signalled, we both shuck our jeans. I could be the 400th man in his bed. This feeling is a bottomless one: I hold the back of his head; he shrugs. As if shrugging's a joke. Like he could embody 'jerk' right now in some clever way and I'd still know it was a joke. From his shaking skin. From his eyes…of a minor equine. I put his glasses on *The Women's Room*; they begin reading avidly. The other men on my 'husband list' will probably never put out. This man will not say 'give me a baby' tonight. I put my head between his legs like it's three courses: not greedily exactly, but carnivorously. I can fish in him, starfish him, anything at this moment.

That moment – the one where I think I can live with the consequences of anything. Like his saying 'Psychology, n'est-ce pas?' as if knowing I'd murder his armpit next. It's the no faux pas zone. (One many writers desire.) His lips are unavoidable – the wrong side of the road. My heart rides back up from my stomach. I can tell the time from his blood-hum. We go into each other, then back into ourselves, physical's only part of it. (We feel a debt to strangers, a personal expenditure. So many are never strangers.)

Every touch till now has been a relatively subtle punctuation. Exclamation marks are called for – if there's to be more than a pause for thought tomorrow. I imagined him mumbling, 'edit me', and I think the textual's worth working on…He thinks I'm a humble country boy, I'm a sex zombie, reentering the world of emotion via his postbox, or flowerhole tucked down at the ground. It's making me want to change a law, be a father. Go the other way, be a robot. Write pop lyrics with semen on the Lower Town Hall. You're legislating my arse to pieces, he says.

Beautiful Mother

You've always associated the two terms together
partly due to your reading of Schiller; partly due
to your watching of *Kimba*. Kimba sublimates
his mother in the water. You've always thought
your mother a baroque figure. You go into the
forest. You make something from a tree: a book
a club. Material comes from the mother; also
happiness, and therefore beauty. The mother
expects love and finds it, finds it beautiful. The
son cries white tears, imagines them surf, a cliff
an iceberg with beer beneath its surface. The
book says tree or mediation; the club says tree
or mediation. The Virgin Mary is prompted to
speak by the movement of the baby in her womb
She speaks Hebrew: 'הוא בועט כמו ממזר' – 'He
kicks like a bastard'. She defines a kind of
democracy. Her followers meet with her at the
temple. Her son, now twelve, is somewhere
swimming, or sublimating his mother in the
forest. He is a kind of book or club. He starts
drinking wine early; he refuses to go into the
army. He has to go across the border to another
country. He works at a cement factory there
When the men knock off the women dance
with him. He's homesick and drinks whiskey
Eventually he swims back across the border
The trees hang over the river. He can't tell

whether he or they are happy or beautiful; he
sees his mother in the sky. The stars are heavy
dramatic. The army still desires him. There
is book and club mediation. His mother prays
for his happiness. He builds a tower out of
beercans and critics say it's beautiful. So he
builds a whole city and people start to live there
practising a form of democracy. Eventually
the area is annexed by Spain. You tell me all
this, mixing art history together with stories
of your mother. You didn't want to go into the
army either. But it was in the army that you first
found love. It was a secret you kept from your
mother. Your mother was not a cartoon, nor
was she a political or religious figure, yet you
mapped her, in a sense, in the sky. She spoke
about you quite differently. She said that she
had taken you from a tree; it was dark and she
hadn't known exactly what you were, whether
text or weapon or musical instrument. That you
were a wooden boy was a complete surprise

A Letter

I like Spicer too, his lovelorn
Unshaken stance. He rarely
Cleaned his oven either I
Expect. You know how to
Dish with someone in a kitchen.
I discern your desire to croon:
A torch singer in a midnight
Blue gown. All the talk, all
The range – yet we could
Slice the tajine with a knife.
Even the spare bed has croissant
Warmth. You lope in, like
An unmurdered Cossack,
Laughing in the tones God
Gave you. This is a subtle
Meeting, has a subtle electric
Feel. I look young and loving
To you I think (relatively).
A fox died on your head,
But it's clean and smells right.
So you're a lunatic in carparks –
A conceptual hoon; you make
Australian poetry – keep it
From tasting like stale cake.
Sparkling on the escalator, so
Agile; some are born to with-
Hold bad news. Though others

Find you cranky so do I. But a
Charm like a homemade broom
Sticks out too. There's a goodness
That surprises, like a shit-stirring
Nun. There's an impasse: I know
You recognise it, flying over it
Like a friendly vulture. Devotion's
An appealing quality…a qualified
Moodiness: like a lemon detector.
A thinness made for hugging. A
Sunny despair. Is the surf high?
Caught any jellyfish lately?
You've a nuggetiness that reminds
Me of ploughing. Let's have coffee
In Darlinghurst. Post-suburban
Boys are far from nothing to me.
They have chutzpa. Will you make
Spaghetti, like they did in the ranges?
On the boulevards chanting out
Random feelgood phrases; marry
Me not the other doctor, the one
With a collage for a head, or's it
A soccer ball? We know so-and-so's
Got foibles, we know 'Bing' drinks
Cream like skim milk. I don't care
For parties but I'd wash dishes to
Talk to you, don't you know – you're
The reason Rousseau was composed.
To put the politan back in Cosmo.

The trees wish they could whisper
'Fuck off' with that much assurance –
I think if you found your own skull
In the grass you'd give it a boot for
Luck. Yesterday I smelt some graff-
Itti, it was like a native cheese
Melting off the wall of the future.
Hello to those big hearts, north
Of the border: they carry their fish
And chips in a holster. The gaijin
Envy me my folder, xx, love
Mike.

Bush Christie

The strangers and travellers were all in place
Only one of them wore a murderer's face
His name was – Mary Gilmore came in then
Making firm statements about the victim:
Banjo Paterson had always liked him
Apparently he owed Henry Lawson six bob
None could remember him having a job
But a poet will always go easy on a sloth
For reasons of euphony, sense or both
John Shaw Neilson was revising in his head
His attitude relaxed towards the dead –
The croaked (all'd seen a few). Adam Lindsay
Gordon too appeared. The dead bloke
Had been speared and poisoned. The
Latter they found out about later. Except
Of course the poisoner, who sat there
Knowing – but were they the spearer
Also? Who in the room was good at
Throwing, apart from Bennelong? It
Wouldn't be him, he's playing detective:
A too predictable upsetting of fictive
Structure. Lawson had been known to
Loose a billy into the scrub when swinging
It to make tea. He wouldn't poison either
One who owed him money (the IOU
Was well-known and had been larger).
Uncharacteristically quiet was Charles

Harpur thought Bennelong, who had
Himself been speared but never homicidal-
Ly. Ned and Dan Kelly played snooker.
Ned appeared to have breasts but they
Were coconut shells shied away from
Shaw Neilson who'd been playing a
Game of 'horse music' with Gordon.
Ned of course had the track record:
But the deceased was not of the police.
Gilmore was preparing a jack o' lantern –
Something she'd picked up in Paraguay
She said. Probably a lie, and she had a
Strong pumpkin-cutting arm…She
Lit a candle and put it in Jack's head.
Bennelong couldn't eat her bread. Pat-
Erson splashed a little gin at Lawson's
Burning card hand, which could have
Made it worse, but luckily didn't.
Lawson had nodded; his cigarette
Caught the edge of an ace or a card
With a face. It'd been a good one
Anyway, Lawson claimed. Harpur
Raised a brow at the waste of the gin
Though currently convinced that drink
Was a sin and could lead to anything.
Mary Fullerton was looking in the bible
For a letter; while Henry Kendall listened
In order to write about it later. It was tribal –
Bennelong was convinced – he didn't buy

The swaggie tag that'd been stuck to the
Murderee. There was more camaraderie
Under the surface than he cared for. This
Was no knife-fight in a dunny over honour
Or money, but some thick coves hiding in
The smoke of a stove in a Shearer's hut
Where treacle did for bush honey. He
Needed a clue: it was in the woodpile
By the stove – a review of a new book
Of not-so-innocent Austral verse. The
Wind changed and a spear went through
The reviewer – a handy piece of wood
Too it was and confiscated...The news-
Paper was dated a week ago. All claimed
To have been at the beach or the snow
Holidaying, not paying attention to lit-
Erary affairs. They spoke in threes and
Pairs. Where did the Kellys come in then?
They were no more poets than Bennelong
Himself: though 'E' took notes on their
Diction. The case became one of dereliction.

Settlers, Regurgitated

Victoria's first settlers were whalers as well
as prostitutes. They were hale, they drank
ale. They were whalewrights, sexwrights –
they were Whites. They ate a lot of pasta
too, well before the Italians put in an appearance.
They didn't call it pasta, they called it boiled
hay. The famous hay-twirlers of that time
have unforch been forgotten, their names deimagined.
By the way, citizens, to give them the retrospective
respect they so often misreceived in their
day, were often waylaid by hayrides heading
to sexpots to prosecute a beached whale for
trespassing. There were lists of such carryons
and possibilities: if you could read and they
could write. The punning laws were the most
like a minefield, to keep in mind. Requirements
and avoidances, speeches and acts: regarding
choir mints, or boy dances, peaches under
the axe. Our most senior writers were born
out of this malaise. You might substitute
scenic or add mayonnaise at this point – but
don't hurt yourself, and don't fall – history
isn't worth it. We had a septic tank once
but who has them or wants to hear about
them now when society is so shit-free? How
they produced any progeny escapes me like
a three-footed convict, that is, awkwardly

that is, confusingly, with so much seafaring
and the unreliability of work. The big stations
where the trains never came. Where they
were forced to invite the black milkman and
the black mailman in in order to enjoy company.
The settlers used to receive a lot of Aboriginal
people back then when wages were more
conceptual (as they're becoming again). There's
something about this narrative that doesn't
make sense! It's like the old days when the
fruit from the sheep got mixed in with the
sultanas: I think I've been talking about New
South Wales half the time – and that's the
most actionable law in the book.

An Australian Comedy

He's learning to see other men as third person cinema
latent with photographs; the laughter knife in the lost jar
He's brought his dog with him, sophomoric thing to do
but they're inseparable, like glass. A grasshopper lands
on the robot's instructions and the clothes are grasshoppered
for a week. A timeless street is rezoned and crumbles
George is here from Singapore, wants to know where
the place to be is; if it's Asian friendly. You are ageing
with your hands in your pouch, your strong tail a seesaw
If the reader is willing to decide what's missing, the question
remains: whether to fill the void or expand it? We differ
but I have better sportswear. Turn around: bell is dell
belong is Geelong. The horses are running, their tongues
and hooves all part of the assembly. You see the old
photographs in your lover's face, and let go of the school
boy's hand; you're growing up again. It turned out there
was a god behind that tree, and we talked a bit about it
The ferry came. They say they don't know, yet make noises
at night, like possums swallowing loads of ants and throwing
them up again. A wicked waste. There in the bed, in the middle
yet somehow separate, lie Sartre and Beauvoir. George
finds a piece of shade shaped like Finland, and lies down
on a buckthorn. The dog orders curry through the record player
but it never arrives. The flags say 'Help! We Are Out Of
Musicians!' The Rolling Stones arrive to talk about their glass
making hobby. A grasshopper lies down in shade the shape
of Broadway or else the head of John the Baptist. What planets

are the best for poets to be born under? The wryness knife
in the temporary jar. He let theatre speak for him: folly
mortology, a jumper that claims to read Thomas Hardy
but really just follows the plot. Ordinary, Index, Insult
and Injury, their noble values are debatable. He was looking
for Asian spinach in a non-Asian grocer's. What's missing
is inevitably there. The goat farm was forced to wear a mute
button, though it was the smell their neighbours went to war
over. The poem stretches like an apple

compose using conceptually thin words

was the screen advice. The rabbit
and badger: both heraldic animals of England, both associated
with unpleasant talk. After dinner, we wait for the billy
to babble, filling our mouths with dread, which is good
for the drain. If a forest creature, like a sentence…A
Japanese nephew, called

the Japanese

gave them Gertrude Stein every Christmas, fearing that
Samuel Beckett would be too gloomy, too goat-farmy
For the same reason he never included them on links
to news stories about police officers bashing people
to death. The gay one made counting uncomfortable
and the resourceful Anglicans invented a new number
half-two. Half-two seemed to embody the
NultimAteulTimateUltimateRultimAteuLtimate

state for people, and evoked for George the novel by
Frederick Rolfe, *Desire in Pursuit of the Whole*. Your
name, as they say, here. The tracksuit lies down in
the shadow of a porridge truck and is stained by a passing
koala. Following the tenets of minimalism, you remove
the stirrup from the pancake. It tastes fine without it
Every line on his lover's face invites him on an eerie
journey. There's an Anglican phoneline that flatters
the over forties

> Press half-two to hear you look just over thirty

Every day he drops an orange on something
nothing learned about that. It's acting like a possum in
a tree without a tree. The leafblower came. What a waste
of ants! He came home to find Divine in the shadow
of the garbage bin. He was snoring the tune of 'Waltzing
Matilda

> gnuch gnuch gnuchgnuch gnuuuuchhh gnuch gnuch
> gnuchgnuch gnuuuuchhh

but on waking claimed to not know the song. The smell
of dog food came through the speakers but no one thought
to turn the record off. The flags say, 'Help! We Are Out
of Daddy Cool!' and Mondo Rock come and talk about
those early days, by the River of Babylon, of cowboy
hats and Molly Meldrum, when every mother wanted a
gay one under a gay sun – all the while knitting with boot

polish. Mars shines down on the grasshopper in its bowl
The trouser knife in the bedroom jar. He was hot and small
like a haiku in a microwave. George had to undress him
just to stop the windows steaming. So many kinds of
cabbage the English have: shiny cabbage, poor cabbage
park cabbage I think…Really? Many kinds of quack too

English

quack

Scots

quack

Australian

quack

American

quack

The

Goat Wanted

poster stretched around the apple tree, so it was spared
Texts before progress is a saying. The merlion is Singapore's

heraldic animal but, like the rabbit and badger, there is no
taboo against eating it. There are several restaurants in
Chinatown where you can get a merlion toasted at your table
They make good yard pets as long as you have a pond
After fifteen cups of tea you feel like a string of bucks that
dusk for money in the twilight. Listening to the tragedies
issuing from the cathedral and throwing in joke grenades
The stirrup spoon stirring in the pancake jar. He licks it, his
tongue like an exploding cocoon. His feet act like possums
a waste...The dog is miming

The careless whistle of a good friend

The flags say, 'We Want Overtime!' and refuse to even
cast shadows on the poor swaggie lost in the twenty-first
century. Some say he used to be an Anglican bishop
but he seems to have a dignity about him as he tries to
buy a cabbage online

It's a beauty for the right people

the ad says. But it sounds like duty and it tastes like it
too. Australians like to see alternative farm animals
turkeys, donkeys, it's too boring otherwise, driving
down the information highway seeing dog deejays now
turned swaggies with their records under their arms, that
they heat up over campfires waiting for a track to spin
them to perdition or wherever you go in a secular universe
Poetry anthologies pile up by the side of the internet, rusty

as a prayer belt while witches dance around them in army uniform

> One thing about the army is you don't get to go to art
> galleries much. If you're on leave you can duck into the
> big museums but you miss those little galleries. That's
> where it's all going on. And you know, so often the big
> ones are undergoing renovations just while you're in town

The war dead lie down in the shadow of the goat farm
A bunyip reclines on its non-novel reading arm. It's
probably just a pig showing off. Two larrikins – they
have a knifely charm – are there on a date

> What're yer into, mate

they say like a couple of badly translated flags, or figs
Grasshoppers wait confidently for the syrup

An Oral Poem

Have you been to the temple?
No, I've never been.
I like the passing of flowers and flame.

An oral poem had come to me in the form of a man.
The poem thought itself strange and hid its own name.
Slightly balding with the kind of mouth an oral poem
needs (to be successful).

You didn't know these things. Your poem was mostly
numbers (and deflection). It stayed with you. It didn't
pour out like an excess of wealth. It wasn't popular,
like oral poems were said to be, nor was it especially
religious. I had been to the temple – not the poem. The
poem couldn't see itself: it was writing. It had innovated
in having been a photo before being a poem. Yet it bore
no developing traces I could see. It was ordinary, but
felt it couldn't be read. You have a PhD, you can read
modesty, it said. I didn't mean to objectify the man or
the poem. I didn't mean to represent my bed as a field:
it wasn't a field. There was no publishing going on…
some flux perhaps…some giving and taking…like a
colonial's word, like an invader's word. The oral poem
was more like a letter than a song; or a diary written
to fit the page. Page, book, these were the concepts we
fell back on. My room reflected my culture. Yet within
this space of abandoned reading, where a laptop served

to transport men, from say, Coburg to Fitzroy, an oral poem was going on. There was drunkenness, but that was, I'd have said, in the margin, rather than in the poem itself...It was in the binding...or the cells: a drunkenness that was both oblivion and self-knowing. Pronouncing 'sigh' like 'sign', an oral poem wondered if its final form was still to come. 'It's coming out quickly', said the poem, but 'it' was not the poem.

Abstract Alcohol

Alcohol brings out the emotion in his voice,
and makes me sentimental about the alcohol.
What is your name? Simone Weil: 'evil consists
in action'. Blood comes out of my sneakers,
I cough up pistachios like an icecream churn
at a wreckery. Things have changed – we've
been reorchestrating in Spain. Severe Spain:
like a pack of dogs entering a convent, throwing
salt on the threshold, pepper on the cat. On
the altar, a gold soccer ball. Green mandolins
recline on the pool table. Think of an RSL
lined with red velvet, a country singer eating
shards of Diamanda Galas records. Curtains.
An old man enters wrapped in violet gas,
shooting sand from his eyes. The country
singer takes off his moss jacket, revealing
a bitumen vest and tattoos like giant staples
down his biceps. A million yellow grasshoppers
stamp their feet and the tail falls off a plane
overhead. ABBA are dead. Their skeletons
perform in the carpark without instruments,
scraping out requests through holes in their
chests. The audience tear at their lamé, bump
against the black Cortina rearview mirrors.
There's no clapping.

I WAS 5 MUM WAS 27 MUM WAS 27 SIMON WAS 3 TINA WASNT B
WAS 26 TINA WASNT BORN SIMON WAS 3 EMMA WASNT BORN
SIMON WAS 3 DANNY WAS 1 EMMA WASNT BORN TINA WASN
DANNY WAS 1 I WAS 5 SIMON WAS 3 I WAS 5 MUM WAS 27 DAN
WAS 27 MUM WAS 27 SIMON WAS 3 TINA WASNT BORN EMMA W
WASNT BORN SIMON WAS 3 EMMA WASNT BORN DANNY WAS
DANNY WAS 1 EMMA WASNT BORN TINA WASNT BORN MUM W
WAS 5 SIMON WAS 3 I WAS 5 MUM WAS 27 DANNY WAS 1 DAD W
27 SIMON WAS 3 TINA WASNT BORN EMMA WASNT BORN SIM
SIMON WAS 3 EMMA WASNT BORN DANNY WAS 1 SIMON WAS
EMMA WASNT BORN TINA WASNT BORN MUM WAS 27 SIMON
WAS 3 I WAS 5 MUM WAS 27 DANNY WAS 1 DAD WAS 26 I WAS
WAS 3 TINA WASNT BORN EMMA WASNT BORN SIMON WAS 3 I
3 EMMA WASNT BORN DANNY WAS 1 SIMON WAS 3 MUM WAS 2
BORN TINA WASNT BORN MUM WAS 27 SIMON WAS 3 MUM W
5 MUM WAS 27 DANNY WAS 1 DAD WAS 26 I WAS 5 DAD WAS 2
WASNT BORN EMMA WASNT BORN SIMON WAS 3 DANNY WA
WASNT BORN DANNY WAS 1 SIMON WAS 3 MUM WAS 27 I WAS
TINA WASNT BORN MUM WAS 27 SIMON WAS 3 MUM WAS 27 I
WAS 27 DANNY WAS 1 DAD WAS 26 I WAS 5 DAD WAS 26 DANN
BORN EMMA WASNT BORN SIMON WAS 3 DANNY WAS 1 MUM
BORN DANNY WAS 1 SIMON WAS 3 MUM WAS 27 I WAS 5 TINA
WASNT BORN MUM WAS 27 SIMON WAS 3 MUM WAS 27 EMMA
27 DANNY WAS 1 DAD WAS 26 I WAS 5 DAD WAS 26 DANNY WAS
EMMA WASNT BORN SIMON WAS 3 DANNY WAS 1 MUM WAS 2
WAS 3 TINA WASNT BORN EMMA WASNT BORN SIMON WAS 3 I
3 EMMA WASNT BORN SIMON WAS 3 DANNY WAS 1 MUM WAS
WAS 3 TINA WASNT BORN EMMA WASNT BORN SIMON WAS 3 I
3 EMMA WASNT BORN SIMON WAS 3 DANNY WAS 1 MUM WAS

MA WASNT BORN SIMON WAS 3 DANNY WAS 1 MUM WAS 27 DAD
WAS 1 SIMON WAS 3 MUM WAS 27 I WAS 5 TINA WASNT BORN
MUM WAS 27 SIMON WAS 3 MUM WAS 27 EMMA WASNT BORN
1 DAD WAS 26 I WAS 5 DAD WAS 26 DANNY WAS 1 I WAS 5 MUM
RN SIMON WAS 3 DANNY WAS 1 MUM WAS 27 DAD WAS 26 TINA
WAS 3 MUM WAS 27 I WAS 5 TINA WASNT BORN SIMON WAS 3
MON WAS 3 MUM WAS 27 EMMA WASNT BORN DANNY WAS 1 I
AS 5 DAD WAS 26 DANNY WAS 1 I WAS 5 MUM WAS 27 MUM WAS
3 DANNY WAS 1 MUM WAS 27 DAD WAS 26 TINA WASNT BORN
AS 27 I WAS 5 TINA WASNT BORN SIMON WAS 3 DANNY WAS 1
UM WAS 27 EMMA WASNT BORN DANNY WAS 1 I WAS 5 SIMON
S 26 DANNY WAS 1 I WAS 5 MUM WAS 27 MUM WAS 27 SIMON
AS 1 MUM WAS 27 DAD WAS 26 TINA WASNT BORN SIMON WAS
TINA WASNT BORN SIMON WAS 3 DANNY WAS 1 EMMA WASNT
MA WASNT BORN DANNY WAS 1 I WAS 5 SIMON WAS 3 I WAS
WAS 1 I WAS 5 MUM WAS 27 MUM WAS 27 SIMON WAS 3 TINA
WAS 27 DAD WAS 26 TINA WASNT BORN SIMON WAS 3 EMMA
ASNT BORN SIMON WAS 3 DANNY WAS 1 EMMA WASNT BORN
SNT BORN DANNY WAS 1 I WAS 5 SIMON WAS 3 I WAS 5 MUM
WAS 5 MUM WAS 27 MUM WAS 27 SIMON WAS 3 TINA WASNT
DAD WAS 26 TINA WASNT BORN SIMON WAS 3 EMMA WASNT
BORN SIMON WAS 3 DANNY WAS 1 EMMA WASNT BORN TINA
BORN DANNY WAS 1 I WAS 5 SIMON WAS 3 I WAS 5 MUM WAS
5 MUM WAS 27 MUM WAS 27 SIMON WAS 3 TINA WASNT BORN
AS 26 TINA WASNT I WAS 5 MUM WAS 27 MUM WAS 27 SIMON
AS 1 MUM WAS 27 DAD WAS 26 TINA WASNT BORN SIMON WAS
AS 26 TINA WASNT I WAS 5 MUM WAS 27 MUM WAS 27 SIMON
AS 1 MUM WAS 27 DAD WAS 26 TINA WASNT BORN SIMON WAS
AS 26 TINA WASNT BORN SIMON WAS 3 EMMA WASNT BORN

The Bon Vieux Temps

He was nothing new (that's why we liked him). He was a
good French
bushman who wouldn't betray a Christian – should you
decide to treat him
like a gently nurtured dame leaping blackberry canes.
Toujours gai: now
the abode en permanence has arrived and nights like
champagne cream fall
distinctly on the ear. We would abstract body parts like
that then (star
illimitable, ocean-brightened). It was Arabian on the
beach. Molonglo
took the bungalow while I lay openmouthed under the
gooseberries. We didn't
call them lady adjuncts then and didn't need to. We
thanked Allah for
the caravanserai or fountain of youth. And it could all go
on with a black
boy to help with the accounts but what if we decentred
Rolf Boldrewood's
sentiments and looked where we were headed, to WWI,
for example.
It was natural to be involved like strawberries in a
washing machine,
if strawberries were innocent of being colonial: but that's
hardly possible
their tendrils get in everywhere.

The Influence Of Lorca In The Outback

Where they once ate camel grease (and before
that I don't know), they now eat moon butter. Where
they once drank electric guitar (and sometimes
acoustic guitar) they now drink lightning. They
talk about the Spanish Civil War as if it happened
just around there, just over there. The Outback's
too large a temple for a Christ. They're always
writing poems about the hot snow of suffering –
or odes to roosters. These are the reports we hear.
They go looking for bones to talk to, like Lorca
was a character in Hamlet. Of course, it could just
be a living analogy: a clinamen in attempts at Indigenous
and European reconciling. At one school in South
Australia, the girls were so taken with *The House
of Bernarda Alba* that it became a cult, enacted
day and night, its themes and narrative infecting
the girls' mothers and other women. There was
much wearing of black (or green, with straw) of
stylised repressive and rebellious gesture (but mercifully
no shooting). It's said that elderly Aboriginal women
would suddenly run into the street saying they wanted
to be married and have lots of children. The play
had become a feminist masque, and spread across
state borders. In one town in New South Wales
the whole male population donned Southern European
mourning drag in order to not be left out. But this
attracted too much media, and the women all went

into the hills until the men put their jeans back on. The many graves of Lorca scattered throughout the desert and in oblique spots on towns' outskirts have become shared sacred places. Even in the cities it's known the Outback is no monoculture; whispers have been heard of resistance, especially by men who find Lorca too feminine. It's said that, here and there, the influence of Rimbaud is beginning to show. That the Paris Commune is referred to as a local moment; while many teenagers wear wrist bandages, and travel the continent on foot. Still others are living more reclusive lives in the style of Dickinson: collecting native flowers, wearing white, and making packets of poetry.

Check The Motor

I like a guy to be a bit cold in love.
To be a chain and drink champagne.
Do you feel like a bit of chicken? Were
you in the ditch with the other one
catching the pneumonia? We were at
Larch Place at the time. Chandra had
'had' a baby, and his father had died
in that tragic accident: a lot of training
back and forth, and a lot of merry
chanting, it being December. The porridge
and the rice went up the chimney, and
the police made him fetch the water.
I went to Poland. Didn't have much
chance, took it on the chin. A pin changed
into a pinch without too much trouble.
The French were all I had. Plenty of
money, naturally. The cheroot became
popular, and a dance called 'the twitch'.
Even a twit could manage it. The coral
were thriving: with the chain of our
help. And with the rain, everything
got pretty cheap, and mixed in with
everything in the fridge, and the mould
and much drinking and generally being
informal. The weak barman acted like
a poor chimpanzee with a lip going
for a buck at a market. For peace –

indeed for the central narrative of Jacob
and the peach pie that everyone wanted
to forget. Men and women who will
torment you for flat feet, and who can
put you in an early grave, try.

being a poem that contains none, though it does have
a HAHA under its seat, and a HAHAHA in its 'avant
garde sleeve' (quoting Kate Fagan, my old tea buddy –
tea for *teannis*, or *teable tennis* – such words bearing
no relation to mine to Kate: unless it be to her mimetic
ability). (This is sounding like a poem by Ken Bolton
II. References to friends a la precedent ('a la Perec' gave
me 651 results, including the information that Perec joined
the Oulipo in 1967, an influence, according to one observer,
that was poison in Calvino's case – not, if someone is
reading this on another planet, that Perec and Calvino
were friends of mine – yet in a sense they are now)
are part of the structure – of a certain kind of poem,
if you went to the New York School, which is all or
at least some of my favourite classes were, about friends –
which might (have once) be(en) thought indulgent or
pretentious or in poor taste to mention or indeed have
but that's not the kind of mistake I could've made 'which
is why I'm telling you about it'. What then becomes
of my own subject (or topoi) if I'm actually building
or evading an argument?) There must be a chicken eating
rubber or a dog saying 'Darling, I just had this new
flea treatment –'. (To be comic that is, not necessarily
in order to imitate Ken Bolton.) (Asides are essential
however.) The tinkle of Mozart cordial at the bar; someone
Asian speaking Harlem jive to a white person from a
suburb (the latter image's arse trademarked in Australian

poetry since before we had arses, in that sense) who's
smiling and looking up jive on their phone. It's always
sunny in a funny poem: I guess a poem 'alone' can
be a comedy? What poem really has a bad ending?
('Imperial Adam.') Poems that choke, for two, which
could bring the less sympathetic reader to ascribe the
tragic(al) to the poet. Getting back to the meteorological
it could be that a poem's bad weather's ironic, or, alternatively
(that tendentious and arguably mendacious adverb; and
why do I say 'or' – does 'or' ever not offer an alternative?
As in 'Would you like milk or milk with your cup or
mug? I'm sorry sir, we're all out of glasses') a backdrop
to a yellow elephant being mistaken for a bus as it loses
its footing in the ice and begins to slide downhill...Not
that its would-be passengers are short of brain or poor
of eyesight, but there's a storm coming – it's dark – they're
desperate. You just have to mention the sun and it lights
up: it thinks it's going to get a chance to talk. It's the
Sesame Street influence. Any particular weather suggests
a scene (the Poetry scene), but who cares? Theories
probably don't know what a parsnip is. For now till
the show actually starts, it's that hammer handle...which
they'll need for building the set. A comedy always has
the fatal sense of inevitability, like the narrator's possessed
of some flaw: such as the need to mention Christopher
Brennan about now (or any auto-undermining French
phrase, 'tour de force', for example). See how deflating
that was? Now we're never going to lose our virginity
or get that interesting disease the doctor tells us ten years

later was a misdiagnosis. How does Ken Bolton maintain
that 99% consistent tone? Is it his sunniness, the mock
bad weather that clouds his brow like a bang – 'if we
still had' bangs 'or' KAPOW's 'that is'? I have a stock
of these expressions, young fella (I don't know about
you, but to me f-e-l-l-a rhymes with colour not stellar,
and / but 'fulla' suggests someone full – of themselves,
or beans, at least, not some co-laconic offsider) that
I keep in my saddlebag. I used to be a bush butcher or
a journalist and I always keep a pinch of drought in
my coin pocket to remind me of the dry anthologies of
colonial writing. You lean forward to smell the joey and
it shoots you in the face with nostalghia (with an 'h'
to remind you of Russian movies of Italian pea pickers
written by 'Oscar Wilde'. Okay I'm conflating 'facts'
here but this isn't actually being written by (the) KBII,
that sturdy if / because unbuilt shipwreck). There's no
need for images to accumulate in this way, as if readers
tend to laugh when they don't get a chance to catch what's
going on – grammar per favore – but rather, it can be
as starkly uncomfortable as a mailbox whistling on a
hilltop, the face of Ezra Pound recognised in a beetroot,
a 'Howdy do?' proffered to a jelly wearing a badge. But
that's to cumulate again. And one uncomfortable reader
laughing doesn't make a comedy (unless *they're* the smart
one in the room). Animals, juxtapositions: it's basically
Surrealism without political (or psychological) intent
(in other words that typical mix of reaction and naiveté –
is naiveté – or naivety – kinder than ignorance, as a description?).

The mule leans back in its comfy chair made of pancakes,
molasses dripping like blood from its jowls, while you
recline on a couch made from your parents' skeletons
and the tricycle you had stolen when you were three...
Now the mule leans forward, and asks how you feel about
getting sexual advice from a mule while you cast around
in your mind for liberal views on mules as expressed in reviews
of American novels, while Alfred Hitchcock goes down
on a window-washer outside. Superficial allusions (what
would an in-depth allusion be? A hoax? *The Arcades
Project*?) to other cultures are just par for the trade, as
are puns, such as 'Zelig-wrestling', 'a Slessor mortal',
or, life under Margaret Thatcher was like being ruled
by Teri Hatcher-as-Susan-Mayer's grandmother: as a
traffic cop with a headache. (Bree, basically. I share
my birthday, 3rd October, with *Desperate Housewives*
and Gore Vidal). These devices usually come in threes
(cue Kirsty MacColl: 'We're not looking for a new England'
or 'We're on the beach' or even 'They don't know about
us' the last covered by comic Tracey Ullman. This style
is really a trap, I was once commended on my ability
to get out of poems – by Kevin Killian, the third 'K'-
initialled poet in this poem) like a triangle, janglingly.

The Structuralist Cowboy

Sort of, meaning exactly. One cowboy rode a frog
another wore a cowpat hat. This was not on a range
nor even a ridge. Whether they rode in from the
crossroads of Trivia, or from a dry spot in New
South Fuckmyarse, was ever discussed. Aaiiee! might
just be the Apocalypse squealing. I wrestled with
my father: the thought that he was John Ashbery
gave me the extra strength to lay him on his back.
I then dragged his godforsaken Gertrude Steinish
hide to the tree in the orchard that opposed the
tree in another orchard I had read about. That was
pure instinct I believe. One cowboy I know liked
to say that the station he worked on was bigger
than Deconstruction. He read Corbière and Marx
in the cowboy editions but by the time they reached
him cowboy was an extinct language. They still
managed to infect him with syphilis, however.
It didn't bother me none: I was horny enough to
give Henry Parkes head if there was anything left
of him to give it to. Oath oath croaked the frog-
steed and the cowpat-owl-hat. What is a cow? How
many per cowcart? On Coney Island is a fence
that keeps the rabbits from drowning, with the
bonus of preventing infestation by water-coneys,
and the resultant lowering of genetic stock, including
in humans. A cowboy kiss is the swallowing of
a rabbit and spitting out the skin. Any damage

to the skin or cowboy and the action can't be called
a kiss but rather a cowboy choke. A leather-bound
volume, that is, a book, may be substituted if the
cowboy has the requisite saliva. In fact an idea
or controversy does as well. Where do I meet all
these people? At the Homosocial Ball of course!
I flounce-galumph in: Cleopatra c'est bush moi
a treesnake gnawing at my breastplate (blue willow
pattern). If I'm an extreme, Shakespeare's a medium
connecting my reality to that of the watertank Lears
lapelled with fourleaf clovers and to the black cowboy
on the Appaloosa, an Othello. A conservative poem's
one that insists on its ending; to avoid such an effect
encode something in the middle or pretend to.
But how do lines – if I may appeal to you directly
for a moment – how do lines enclosed as they
are (if sentences) between stops – and if not, then
separated by breaks – know what other lines consist
of? If we deny author control isn't textual autonomy
suggested as much as that of reader? Theme is
extinguished. Lines read each others' minds. Cowboys
don't just ride onto the page or screen unconnected
and uninvited. The chances of them stripping down
to shower outside are also perhaps slim. But
it's dusty riding and water restrictions have ended
albeit with caveats to be sensible. Group showering
encouraged; reading of dust and sweat trails: of
situations not unlike that of the arrival of foreign
warriors, thirsty and weirded out. Henry Parkes

finds his oasis; others, younger, more powerfully
built, not so lucky. 'I'm a radio' on a window ledge
as they ride into town, 'dark clouds above' them.
Riding, dialling. The station like a beach as big
as psychoanalysis. Cowboys have a lot of baggage.
They make interesting patterns in the sand.

Spoiled For Choice: 80 Ganymedes

Springtime Simon on a park bench;
Beau, like a telephone pole in blossom.
Claude's his own cloud, brow furrowed like a poem –
Lissome Liam: any god would lose something for him.

If the sweetness of Dean was a powder you'd snort it.
And Don is a sure thing for later on.
Seth would put the god of death in love mode,
The step of Stephen *is* light as a hen!

I'd like a witness like Marvin, get me?
A lyric in speedos, also known as Ben.
Ross in white apron, with cheeks of rose,
A thought made flesh, and named Theo.

The body of Craig wasn't made for work;
Rupert in green wraps well, like a snake.
Sean is sharp, but of a dull family.
Jim provokes a longing in the pants.

Who wouldn't take Hugh to a mountain hotel?
Leave the lawn unmowed for a month with Jay?
Dorian's a cause to go marching for;
The internet's crammed with such wealth as Mitch.

The gods gathered at Alex's unveiling.
They forgave Max his hair like a cypress.
Flynn's always first in his onlooker's hearts.
But it's '2r' Garry has the magic touch.

Teddy like the others beyond beauty's formulae,
Jack on the stairs – a vision to behold!
A god stole Ivan from a nightclub cage,
But regretted sweet Roy as they passed his room.

Luke is idle, except for his lashes,
Oscar has a lapdog with dyed green ears.
Harry, though poor, has a formal aspect;
Yoshi is always being chased by bees.

Ahmad has a hedge he prunes when topless,
Luigi's a still-life with apple, fish.
We all want the key that Troy is holding;
Marshall shades his eyes with his hand and we die.

If Zac is human, gods are lesser beings.
If Paul's a fabric, I'd like a new suit.
The sighs of Cedric would set a train weeping,
And Xavier's gold hair make an alchemist despair.

Scott's hair is darker – it sets off his parka,
Drew makes all the wolf gods go woof.
Trent's rented his body but it looks brand new;
Notice Jared: you're already in heaven.

Raph and Gabe are twins and bad angels both;
Dougie treads water like a dolphin.
Ricky aspires to go into orbit –
My every last hope is in Dane.

Glen is elegant – look at his bones!
Billy would give an elephant nerves.
Tony accepts the burden of an ever-ringing phone,
Butterflies feast on Obie's breath.

Ty has tasted love: you can see it in his eyes.
The ripple of Nick's back starts a panic.
When Aaron is smiling it changes the light,
While Adam is as slippery as a calf.

The city competes in beauty with Louis
Olivier is cunning but on balance, generous;
Juan thinks pocket combs are forever,
And everyone's praying Dylan's back soon.

Bobby likes to spend Wednesday alone.
When Conor winks the trees shake off their leaves.
Cornelius eats sour things – he likes to pucker;
Dom is perfect in almost all departments.

Tan loves miming: for example, the horizon.
Serge likes to think he's an action feature.
Colm stands straight – like a prize for crying;
Francois was taken by an eagle, but dropped, unhurt.

Brandon always wears felt.
There is nothing softer than Eugene's nature.
Kurt likes to add snow to a drink;
George looks tough but is delicate.

Daniel delights in the mockery of bugs;
Rocky has a lot of 'go'.
A sunset is lacking without the company of Yves:
Todd adds panache to the frame.

No one wears a fringed jacket like Dino.
Sylvester's still happiest by water.
Raoul is restless: like an antelope that wants
To be eaten. I'm the replete big cat.

ben 6 ways

1 He can snap his fingers like a hood. he
2 Possibly his tongues a bit thick.
3 He says uhoh / horror / a pickle
4 he likes broadway. the restaurants
5 chewy. ummm – kneehigh to a kiwi? he
6 dramas. Thats his clear-sky nature,

1 kicks the bed when nervous…a musical hi
2 He will give you a kiss out of nowhere
3 . its not hard to make him laugh
4 busy, so it must be funny
5 watches chinese family dramas,
6 i havent seen him drunk since. he

1 comes out of his hello-box. so
2 . hello, this is nintendo speaking
3 . he likes his ballet, &
4 . gulp, cold drinks, something
5 but doesn't read chinese; lives malaysian family
6 tells his sister, not his aunties

In Bed With Metallica

She moves out of the painting like a metal
Band…She's carrying the frog of darkness
The crowds, the Parisian crowds are forming
And it makes me weep. I buy a jigsaw puzzle
To support the industry. I don't need something
To do in my hotel room: I just need fame
And a frame and someone under glass to visit
At 3am. It's got to be Leonardo da Vinci
Sketching naked rehearsing members of
Metallica. He doesn't know photography's
Invented – and no one wants to break his heart.
Or tear him apart to find the secret of his genius.
We read him Berrigan's sonnets: he thinks it's
Standard English – and that T. Rex is a fragrance.

Dirty Harry Is Scorpio

Rectangles are blue. He takes the mirror
and laughs at bureaux, at partnerships. Bus
under bridge, hair flowing wild. Cereal
watching, TV munching, did you expect
that milky fuzzing? It's no one's fault. If
the bullet can't be found, we're mere roulette

Every cent, every mayor is on death

You're better off on the moon, stay put, stow
your gun in an empty crater, learn to
love junk or a footprint. I want to be
that high relief shadow, that cool slice of
decision: you should head home. The banks move
in and out of access, the church desires
to be somewhere high, bright and undestroyed

The Great China Draggers

Why should we object to heartbreak when
it makes our love the stronger? It was one
of those days when the traffic kept veering
into the oaks due to the glare of the neon
displays: elegants smoked thin strips of celery
by their caravan barbecues, and the shrill
honking of zebras disturbed the matronly
teenage boys making up their lists for weekend
squash and pillow biting. Achoo! I was back
in the room, Charles and Emma played cribbage
in the corner, only the fine patina of cocaine
on Emma's nostrils suggested cribbage wouldn't
satisfy the next decade of afternoons…Catherine
designed pages for ads where tiny buffalo
roamed a celery patch, leaving health warnings
on the stalks. Why not just use ants? objected
Heathcliff. Who would take the word of ants –
nay even an army of ants? retorted Catherine,
though she knew from acrid experience her
buffalo would be shot down by marketing.
It was one of those days – tinged with nutmeg –
when small white bulls were harnessed to
large china objects to distract writers from
their publishers' inexplicable delays. Thank
you for your grotesque letter; the receipt
for the anaesthetic was especially numbing…

The rules of cribbage are as follows…Have
I missed anything relevant? The cameleer,
writing in Arabic of his imprisonment in
this drawing room, this mini Hotel California
if you will, addresses himself to the relevant
officer of the State Library of W.A. He wonders
how on earth he'll make his script recognisable
as poetry; sticks sugar violets to the pages,
and infuses, mentally, his purple ink with
the Spirit of Verse. Caterers arrive, and pop
balloons of soup and hot chocolate over the
slack mouths of the guests. They're not paid
to check for pulses! Now that I've destroyed
what I've seen with description, I'll withdraw,
leaving a world, a rumour, a tarpaulin marked
with the muddy tracks of buffalo, who even
now huddle on the edges of the Universe,
to smoke and pray and jab Gatsby in the eye.

Motherlogue

Whenever I start a narrative poem she says *God*
God God, so you can take that for granted: I'm
editing her responses. This is the yarn of, well,
you'll recognise it (and imagine her with her hands
over her ears as she does the washing up: with
her elbows I suppose). After my third there was
a swan and then a suckling pig. I'd find myself
hanging out clothes in my underwear – or my husband's –
and the neighbours drawing the blinds at each other,
saying, she's not really adjusting to Wahroonga
is she? They – inside my own house – have eaten
me a hole in the couch, and I'm doing the accounts
with one hand and killing a snake with another
while I get an armful of wood. But after a few wines
and a few accidental discounts 'at' work (I have
an online business) I'm ready for Joint Family
Suicide: one of our 'TV games'. *God God God*
adding rhythm. Then my eldest comes in with blood
on his face from fighting with some Pymble trash
and says we're out of water. So I gather up the
tribe: one or two boys, one or two girls, the swan
and the suckling pig, and we head towards the
Lindfield reservoir, each of us with the biggest
water vessel we can carry. Then there's a shift
in critique, she's saying *you can't*, meaning I can't,
tell a woman's story. But I am telling it. Mariah
(named after the wind, not the singer) has crawled

into a crocodile, and I didn't even know they had
crocodiles on the North Shore, but I'm only a girl
from Nimmitabel with a horde of kids of one kind
or another walking the edge of the road, wine bottles
in hand playing sweet, sweet music with their little
breaths. The swan gets in after her, and I wouldn't
want to be a crocodile on the other end of a swan.
I think the swan left a torn Coke can in the croc
for good measure. And Mariah comes out all slimy
and beaming with some sorry overbred excuse
for a Wahroonga hound, saying, Mummy, look
I found a puppy! And I say hooray, what are you
going to feed it on? But there's a crow eating a
possum as we turn the corner, and Mariah's got
her waddy so she shoos the crow on the head and
puts it in her dilly bag and sets the little socialite
with its faux diamond collar's kisser in the pre-
pecked possum. *Uh, animal cruelty? Examples
to children?* I hear over the lino vacuuming. Bush
rules, I say. It's starting to get dark, and as I'm
new to this builtup area (only having recently moved
here from Belconnen) it seems very strange and
eerie. The houses here truly have no season, no
blossom, and the lawns have no smell. I had a couple
of cones earlier and a slight feeling of paranoia
begins to resurface. But as anyone who thought
of it would say, you can't drink paranoia (let alone
have a bubble bath in it or boil spuds). So we head
on, but I'm glad I brought my shotgun. The kids

and co. are all wearing their scapulas, too. So when
the Devil rides up on a horse, I'm terrified but stand
my ground. Nice little herd of pigs you got, he
says, stroking the dead lamb in his lap. He broke
into my consciousness with that one, I said to Trent
later. I'll give you a waterbag for the boy, he said,
not pointing at my oldest, but at Jess, my androgynous
third, and I said no deal. Give us a billy out of
the good of your heart, I said. And while I waited
on his reply I chanted Hail Mary, full of grace,
the Lord is with thee, and he said Nema eartson
sitrom aroh ni te cnun. Which sounded like nothing
but I soon realised was the Ave Maria in backwards
Latin. And I said, in forwards Spanish, Dios te
salve, María, llena eres de gracia. And the Devil
replied Nema etrom artson alled aro'llen osseda
(in backwards Italian) so I said, grabbing the billy
by the handle as I did so and mentally thanking
the Portuguese nun I'd studied with, Avé Maria,
cheia de graça, o Senhor é contigo. And he grabbed
the handle too with his bony hand like Voss come
out of the desert to steal my children, my honeybees,
muttering in his best better backwards French accent,
Nema trom erton ed erueh'l à te tnanetniam. I shot
half his head off then, yelling fit to rouse the Nazis
from their Master Chefs in Hell, Gegrüßet seist
du, Maria, voll der Gnade, der Herr ist mit dir!
I knew I was out of languages, and I could tell he
was ready with backwards Tagalog. Jess gave me

her / his saw and I cut off the Devil's fingers
and took the billy: it was a diabolical billy and
never emptied. So we threw our bottles into the
bushes and headed home, thinking that Trent would
probably be back from the bank by now. Steeds
of Satan though are faster than lightning, and we
got home an hour earlier than we'd left. So I decided
not to smoke the second time round; gave Mariah
a pot to cook the crow in, and did some journalling.
It looked like we could make ourselves at home
in Wahroonga after all. I can hear exaggerated
yawning from the bedroom, so I'll leave the story
there, put the garbage out and the kettle on and
go into the love of my life. My witchetty's at half-
mast already. Bon voyage-nuit!

What We Understand Went On

She was moaning what sounded very like 'Give me Gertrude
Stein or give me death!' as she went through the clues in her
folder. Her toes were like blue lagoons in an asphalt ashtray;
her brow furrowed like Chinese pasture / pasta. Surprised?
At the checkout, apprised of a different custom (because a
different country), sir beamed a resentment ray at the grapefruit
display, erasing any lingering oxblood tang. 'Are you making
eyes at me?' asked the orangutan. Or was it a recording that
the keeper played for visitors to enjoy? Carmelite nuns smiled
sweetly at the milk-trough and the models got caught in the curd.
Cordelia felt fended off by the mall's nomenclature, and left
cabbageless in fevered distaste. She bought paste. What kind
we don't know, adjectives are sometimes useful, but not necessarily
for making coleslaw without a cabbage. She nutted out 'Coles
law' then. 'What kinds of dudes live around here?' she asked
Basket, her poodle. 'Thirty-eight year old Singaporean jocks
in socks', was the assayance. Archaeopteryx pretty much owned
the carpark. The pavement saucepans banged like there was no
acute hearing. 'Don't turn your back on me, shopping trolley,'
was all she had to say: we were in Philadelphia. Safe pop
aficionados, Boyz II Men started well but turned to treacle, no
Temptations they. There were no earthquakes that afternoon,
even in the movies: so every thoroughfare, every promenade
was chockers with veiled Australians determined to sell something
and not just buy like a fucking bishop all the time. All the good
haircuts she noticed; Brisbanite nuns wrestled airplanes to the
ground, she remembered, from the rodeos of youth. It seemed

a little exaggerated, but she was pretty sure. This was research, tuning into speech patterns, making allegories out of street activity. In an earlier incarnation she had been a street sweeper, but found no more info that way than she did now, as a dog-walking, iPod-fake-listening, pole-kissing, aboveground archivist chick. The doofi had no comeback: barely enough narrative thrust to put their collective backs out. The wangs glistened like snail tracks on a get-out-of-salt-farm. Way up ahead, some militant cottonwool was sodomising an exhaust pipe for its archaisms. It was perhaps Margaret Rutherford. There were no Danish queens keeping the avenues cool. Basket tried to hail a taxi. A few guys in camouflage twisted languorously in the heat. Cordelia had, she thought, no entrée, till Basket coughed up a breadstick that got their attention – they assumed it was armed and hit the ground in a formation unconsciously led by the former star of a highschool Swan Lake, Cordelia surmised. She was hardly Yoko Ono and this was far from being WWII France, so she hoisted herself onto Basket and rode off into the pretzel shop, a kind of downtown backyard, with cinnamon.

California Girls

With their crotches they could crush, we're told,
both the Sydney Harbour Bridge and the Opera
House in one turn of a tanning angle – they've
done it in Los Angeles before. They walk with
high heels on Venice Beach: they could make any
rock platform sand. At fifty still wearing bikinis
while lecturing on Whitehead, brushing students
from their hair. If you've seen Banksy's documentary,
you'll have seen all the corporate cleaners being
processed into bleached pubic bushes for these
giants: other immigrant workers jerking off and
bleeding into vats that broadcast banks of attraction
and resistance to the non-Californian world. If
there's anywhere left that could really be called
that. In San Francisco a young mathematician finds
her homework unchallenging; in Orange County
an athlete pole vaults over a statue of a pierced
navel. She has d y k e tattooed on one set of knuckles
and m a r x on the other. We own them I suppose,
in the way that ownership's dialectic in Western
terms or symbiotic in original Australian. Just
turn on the internet, and you'll see men flaunting
cleavage and Hollywood. They're frog ancestors,
confusing slim for slime. I've been kidnapped by
these Girls; they make me pretend to be gay, force
me to brunch with them, to wear sunglasses as
big as my head, and eat icecream made from something

that doesn't look or taste like milk. We go shopping
for apartments made out of diamantes or cute little
chinchilla farms you can wear as a wrap if a designer
breeze drifts in. Then we play swimming pool Frisbee,
as often as not with gin in the swimming pools
in place of water. We get things done, the things
of our bodies. If this was then we'd be 'My Sharona'.
We star in a commercial for something toxic and
shiny: they have their own planet, why should
they care? At night, in bars, treating men like celery.
The celery responds like it's fleas. How can I and
my brothers crammed in the Girls' backpacks escape
and return home to Japan? Pepsi in Japanese means
California Girls and they have us hooked on the
stuff. But we salt away their collagen until we have
enough to build a Shinkansen. Meanwhile we endure
many hot sessions with Kanye West. We are all
super straight and the sight and smell of his masculine
body is a heavy blow. He shoots his load like putting
out a fire. He will say one worthless thing after
another and then it suddenly coalesces into brilliance:
even his farts syncopate. Once, coming back from
yoga, we are confronted by a protest rally, of beautiful
stumpy women under seven feet tall. Some even
wear glasses, which enrages the contact lens heiress
of our troupe / army. What on earth did they have
to protest about? Who'd bother reading their grubby
matte signs to find out? David Hockney made a
few sketches – we tried to make contact. But he

was hard of hearing or easy of feigning. I think
he thought he was seeing a tsunami as the smiles
of the Girls approached their kitten shakes. They
were perhaps a screen. Mouthy women teens talk
down to them, though they have to climb on Gloria
Steinem to do it. Who will build shelters for them
when they come out of the sun? It's the responsibility
of the community: they can't go back to their own
planet, they've acquired too many shoes. The mathematician
turned physicist hits on using these Girls as the
sun – should the old one fail – or as an ultraviolet
shield. But there's an accident at the factory and
the socialist rags hold their grudging praise for
an exposé. The sun didn't fail exactly; but it got
interested in physics, and concentrated on the beach
less than it had, hanging around the Ultraviolet
Museum in Chicago with Brian Wilson who became
fascinated with the diagrams and recorded a concept
album around them. It rocked everyone's huevos off.

New I New Field

When I was bung, I pursued all kinds of things. I was
a beast, but now I am a beast. That's what Happiness
wants: a beast that reads four pages of *Hebdomeros* a
day. The beast doesn't destroy things, the I destroys.
The I is in the field. Passing rhinos slurp at my soup.
'My' is a semantic compromise. But then so's 'soup' –
and a digestive one. A drug in the soup keeps the rhinos
believing it a form of love. I have points, so don't need
love. I learned points theory growing up in Venezuela.
There may be some inconsistency of representation.
Unstable portal effects. I pursue Z now. I clear the field.
This gets more difficult; I sit at the lunch table, firing
weapons, ordering more soup, interviewing Pink. Only
last year I lost Michael Cera. It was a trap, an attempt
to make me psychologise the environment. A virtual
poet-object, I manoeuvre the ',', the comma-object ,-,-,-,
keeping the waiters coming but ,!, not killing me accidentally.
I lay down pages from Miles Franklin's *My Brilliant
Career*. This discomposes Z. I move the DVD into a
locker, and propose writing the screenplay. The plane
changes. Pink's seat begins to spin. We're on a cloud
declaiming Shelley, 'I change but I cannot die'. I almost
fall out of the plane. On the ground…Z building towers.
ZZZZZZZZZZZZZZZZZZZZZZZZZZZZZZZZZZZZZZZZ

ZZZZZZZZZZZZZZZZZZZZZZZZZZZZZZZZZZZZZZZZ
I…There's a waiter in the distance, a rhino…234860.

Whatd'y'reckon? __ bugger, __ bug. Conversation by the
stump, structured like a romance. Judy Davis swearing.
Davis takes the ball up to the opposition. Kim Hughes
runs a glove through his curls. The smell of super. 'Eyes –
in – the – morning – sun –' I attenuated, Z. The training
ground. The trail of , , , , , , , The Pink interview, titled,
'My Brilliant Car-Z', inspires a video. A trail of , , , ,
rip up Car-Z's tyres. Z explodes. Not the end, no end.
Poetry's the grail. Poetry isn't (in) the field. There has
to be a way to use the object. In order to end the moral
famine and marry the waiter, a range of tactics can be
employed. The helpline admits this. The waiter will then
unfold, revealing themselves to be...(, , , , , spilling out
like ants from a carpet). The rhinos will be broken open,
the soup hardened into...A score will be announced. , ,
, , , , will pour from the machine: a jackpot of minions.
A plane will write in the sky LUNCH + LOVE and DAYTIME
DOESN'T EXIST. A board game will be abandoned.
Still not the end, still no end. Questions will be asked,
mostly irrelevant, how did you get into this fairytale
business? Was it an advantage growing up as younger
brother to the Brothers Grimm, the eighth dwarf, Sleeping
Beauty's twin, Insomniac Beauty? Was there always
a , in your ear, under the mattress, on your spoon? How
did you define yourself against the expectations of the
world? Tear yourself open, the voice said, sounding close
to human...That brute agenda...There were other implications.

Mary (Walk, Assassination, Rendezvous)

If A is predicted then A will happen
or not happen. In other words A and
B are predicted. This logic forms the
basis for the narrator's later boast of
being a soothsayer. Any identity once
claimed sticks to some extent, and
can be used to influence outcomes.
Love is like oxygen after all. At the
narrator's college first year narrators
walk the canal. Walking, as they've
learned, is one of the most common
actions of a character in fiction, and
must be narrated with some familiarity
if not condescension. Mary walks through
the shark-infested sleet trying to work
out whether either or both is real, the
sleet or sharks. It is summer, one of
the four popular seasons. Mary uses
her own name as an avatar. Thus

MARY or MA
RY

She came to understand narration as
a kind of war, from noticing the language
her lecturers used. For example, attacking
the text, defending the narration from

the plot, and vanquishing the author
She recognised the felicity of her name
and reinforced it with an anagram

MARY or MA
ARMY RY
AR
MY

Now she had the beginnings of a bunker,
though hardly a fortress, she activated
her defence field, her M-Ray

MARY or MAR
ARMY YAR
MRAY MYM
RAY

She was required here to practice on the
assigned novels. She got through *Kaputt*,
Catch-22 and *All Quiet On The Western
Front*. She learned a lot about tone
command, about captaining a narrative
She was in short a warrior, with a
battle cry that was MYAR! yelled
suddenly, as one syllable. This was
what she needed – a four letter by four
letter tank of self

MARY
ARMY
MRAY
MYAR

And when she suffered from sharkbite or
missile, and looked something like this

MAR
AR Y
MR Y
MYAR

She merely retrieved extraneous punctuation
from Henry James and rebuilt:

M,A,R,Y
A,R,M,Y
M,R,A,Y
M,Y,A,R

Before the semester was over she had
begun her own illicit novel, which began
'Commas are stronger than you think'
Punctuation acted as portals to other
worlds, where narration was free of
tone, of walking, of character and author

enemies, where narrators could swim
through the snow and fly with the sharks
and Assassination and Rendezvous
were always deferred till next assignment

Transpacific

The view of the watery gardens suggested a *truly*
Verbal rosette. We see the world as a black and
White golf course. Constellations like buttons on
Apollinaire. How much longer can we afford it?
We fall – in performance – in rose coloured costumes
shooooooooooooooorT Paaaaaaaaaaaaaaaaaaaants
Leave your backpack and duty free gin with the
Luggage of the others. Now it's too late to choose
Between a life of Christ or the Buddha. I could hear the
Metal tearing but couldn't see anything in the bathroom
CarrrrrrrrrrrrrroT Piiiiiiiiiiiiiiiiiiie
was the last thing I regretted about my

BOYHOOD
Gosh is not an Australian WORD
Let it wash into the sea SAID
Australian GOD
So many WORD
-s TRACED
from SYD
-ney. WORD
-s that APPEARED
slightly rusty. (It was actually BLOOD

T-Plane; white magic. We use a different number system
And believe that this has improved the area's economy. It
Was a century. It produced a lot of songs. We learnt to draw
On the back of an owl without falling. Now we're slowly edging
Towards Babel in reverse. With a lot fewer languages of course

Eucalypso

Let go the politics
Of this dance
We can't

grass

happens

But art is fire
A

tree

Is a pole of ocean

logging

On to Hawai'i beach

all

The big islands that a Europe can't have
Say them now the names, don't drag it into a game
Thinking

seeds

Burning thoughts
I clean my

teeth

With twig and leaf
Saltwater like mother's hair to us
Stretching my mouth as I reach

the end

A stack of horizons to scan and send
Eucalyptus aforethought
Over the land

mass

Like an interior

mOOn

pulls

The tide in

sOOn

Every field

will

Be covered with cream and

coPPer

Like a cult

Like a sugar plum wind or foam

Not a cloverleaf

Not a

cloveR Rectangle

Gnome

With two clay

feet

The Blazon Family

HAIR OF marmoset /
hair of marmite / hair of margarine
hair of daffodil / landfill / windmill
hair of aniseed / anchovy / anthill
hair of ostrich egg / olive branch / orange peel
hair of sandalwood / candlestick / brass door handle

FOREHEAD OF sphagnum moss / Ian Moss / Kate Moss
forehead of spaghetti / noodles / rice
forehead of chihuahua / gazebo / Tarago
forehead of calamine lotion / calendar sheep / Calamity Jane
forehead of snowmen / mailmen / starmen

EARS OF yoyo / yoghurt / yeomen
ears of Moe Szyslak / Mona Lisa / Moses
ears of Dracula / Batman / Medea
ears of waterfall / strawberries / clocks
ears of whipped cream / stockwhip / whippet

EYES OF billiard balls / billy tea / brilliantine
eyes of corduroy / felt / fat
eyes of drummer boys / doughboys / Joseph Beuys
eyes of choirgirls / showgirls / Elvis
eyes of set squares / town squares / triangles

LIPS OF pickup sticks / chopsticks / stick insects
lips of sea / sky / blue eyes
lips of lunchbox / boxcar / car keys
lips of cardamom / peas / feet
lips of 'A's / apple peel / Lego

TEETH OF granola / juice / radio
teeth of woodgrain / woodstain / piano
teeth of beetles / Beatles / battles
teeth of Mortein / Tina Turner / turnip
teeth of tulips / lizards / brick

NECK OF oxygen tank / piggy bank / Frank Hardy
neck of mountain / iceberg / wave
neck of copperhead / silverbeet / Freddie Mercury
neck of wild roses / wildebeest / Kim Wilde
neck of coffee beans / lima beans / jelly beans

SHOULDERS OF fire alarms / llama / lumberjacks
shoulders of lamingtons / Remingtons / wellingtons
shoulders of bookends / endive / diving boards
shoulders of coffins / chimneys / cars
shoulders of cigarettes / battered fish / Christmas gifts

ARMS OF bracelets / gunpowder / florins
arms of rubbers / pistols / whiteout
arms of pineapple / Venus de Milos / flippers
arms of blockout / stingray / leopardprint handbags
arms of newspaper / unicorns / antennae

TORSO OF dominoes / rooks / aces of spades
torso of flamingo / raven / weathervane
torso of taco / ketchup / forks
torso of potato / Gravox / slate
torso of Coco Pops / cornflakes / prunes

HANDS OF blood plum / truncheon / dole form
hands of stethoscope / 'Vacant' sign / bleach
hands of bourbon / Big Ben / phone booth
hands of slippers / clown nose / faucets
hands of packhorse / tissues / corncobs

HIPS OF pear / kilts / courtesans
hips of amoeba / soldiers / trumpets
hips of glasses / cats / tortoises
hips of cloud / lightning / tornado
hips of curry / chicken soup / milk

GENITALS OF Einstein / Mozart / Mother Teresa
genitals of pipecleaner / daisy / thermometer
genitals of swan / gold / horns
genitals of camera / paintbrush / stiletto
genitals of garlic / compass / balloons

THIGHS OF *Mansfield Park* / *Abbey Road* / *Brighton Rock* DVD
thighs of Helen Mirren / George Harrison / Jane Austen
thighs of sparrow / white mouse / Loch Ness monster
thighs of Monte Carlos / Scotch Fingers / Oreos
thighs of Westminster Abbey / Père Lachaise / Ors cemetery

KNEES OF Michael Jackson aged 5 / 25 / 45
knees of spaceship / watertank / fort
knees of porpoise / eyelashes / KKK
knees of snails / fruit Danish / envelope
knees of clog / willow / bandicoot

FEET OF toothpaste / charcoal / bootlace
feet of campfire / pumpkin / guitar
feet of oyster / moustache wax / couch
feet of haystack / pyramid / monkey
feet of peanuts /
        feet of fossilised fish /
                feet of plasticine Sweeney Reed

Manual

I ’ ve only read marr - iage manuals . The
Bible , Proust , Naked Lunch . They ’ re long , challenging
. You only get one , perhaps two tips from ev
- ery book . But if a poem could give adv
- ice to singles ? Marr - iage being arbitrar
- y , I choose a short poem by Ezra Pound
called ‘Silet’ : ‘ It is enough that we once came
together ’ . That ’ s it for Pound : no problem . Ink
is ‘ immortal ’ , pens are ‘ deathless ’ . This is the
point . Love written down . Love remembered . ‘ What if
the wind have turned ag - ainst the rain ? ’ The turning
isn ’ t the point . Wheth - er you ’ re the wind or the
rain – irrelevant . It ’ s the characterist
- ic ‘ have ’ . Pound ’ s word that the having still exists
: beyond any turn - ing . This isn ’ t a tipon
wedding , still it defines eternal love

seating arrangement

table 1
eldest child of an eldest child and an eldest child
eldest child of an eldest child and a middle child
eldest child of an eldest child and a youngest child
eldest child of an eldest child and an only child
eldest child of a middle child and a middle child
eldest child of a middle child and a youngest child
eldest child of a middle child and an only child
eldest child of a youngest child and a youngest child
eldest child of a youngest child and an only child
eldest child of a only child and an only child

table 2
middle child of an eldest child and an eldest child
middle child of an eldest child and a middle child
middle child of an eldest child and a youngest child
middle child of an eldest child and an only child
middle child of a middle child and a middle child
middle child of a middle child and a youngest child
middle child of a middle child and an only child
middle child of a youngest child and a youngest child
middle child of a youngest child and an only child
middle child of a only child and an only child

table 3

youngest child of an eldest child and an eldest child
youngest child of an eldest child and a middle child
youngest child of an eldest child and a youngest child
youngest child of an eldest child and an only child
youngest child of a middle child and a middle child
youngest child of a middle child and a youngest child
youngest child of a middle child and an only child
youngest child of a youngest child and a youngest child
youngest child of a youngest child and an only child
youngest child of a only child and an only child

table 4

only child of an eldest child and an eldest child
only child of an eldest child and a middle child
only child of an eldest child and a youngest child
only child of an eldest child and an only child
only child of a middle child and a middle child
only child of a middle child and a youngest child
only child of a middle child and an only child
only child of a youngest child and a youngest child
only child of a youngest child and an only child
only child of a only child and an only child

Bringing The 'A'

The ship came bringing the 'A'

The land was read as a space for the 'A'

The 'A' damaged the land and fed the people
Who brought it

In Aboriginal Australia there were no cattle
No cloven: therefore no 'A'

Convicts were whipped with strips of 'A'
Hats too were made

The 'A' roamed everywhere, making itself
Stand for everything (it was consecrated in
Architecture

Aboriginals found the 'A' meaningless
At first – then a means of defence. To
Every assault they returned a Latin 'A'

The 'A' was said to have always been here
Yet they still celebrated the coming of the 'A'
On the ship

The 'A' was in the bush now, it could never
Be caught and sent back, it was
Perhaps not an 'A' any more but
A tree's deformed horns, or a
Rusty piece of rock

The Story Of What's Inside The Heart

When someone's going to kill you, love you, they like
to know what's inside you. I feel like that too and _
don't even know you. I came out of the bush, I put
my hand in the wound in your side (wanting to know
what was there). It wasn't poetry. No 'story' either:
the story was inside the story. The love was defined in
the love: and, looking in – at the ink *in* the ink – I saw
the language that was in language. The Renaissance
in The Renaissance. And it was all there. It was the
wait inside the wait – it was the happening *inside* the
happening. Even Jesus _ when we opened him up
was full of Jesus. That was the case of the case for
many of us, and not so long _ in the not so long ago.
The hurt's still felt in the hurt. The names are still
all inside the names. Not forgetting the crows inside
the cross inside the cross inside the crows...Everyone
wants to know what it means. To fill their knowing
with knowing; to feel the blood inside their blood.
Listen to the song in and of _ the song. I came out of
the radio _ and was a radio. The purity of radio was
other to the purity of songbirds – the birds that flew
into _ and out of being birds. Inside the difference,
difference, they sang; inside the same, the same.
In every country, they found that country. Stuart,
Stuart, Stuart, Stuart. Cooke, Cooke, Cooke, Cooke.
Open him up! There were questions inside questions;
worries coiled in worries. He's going into the clock:

there's a clock there, and it chimes. It ticks! It lies! Lies that have no inside – or outside. Lies that are told by no one, to no one...aren't told at all. They're not *narrated*. According to the face it was in honey, the honey and the face were one, but Jack said...It's for you: you see in what you see. Cubes of meat, cut ever smaller. Glasses of coke, going on forever. 'Come into the house. Come into the house.' See the iron iron iron...There was a self-made spice rack. A guitar, an infinitely alcoholic guitar. When the stars pierce you, when you feel the heart beating in (the heart of) your heart (the stars that are in the stars, the imploding moonlight), when you open yourself up and are all heart, all blood opening, all you, and _ no one knows. They're more concerned with their pockets (yes, full of pockets). Their concern's so concerned, so concerning. Yeah, and there's so much style in style, it's the only thing to eat; spoon by spoon, Stuart by Stuart, heart by mouse by _ little green die...with a skull on it instead of a five. When you throw it you'll know it if _ your alive's still alive.

Order

'The sacred is order'
Like pyramids; Akhenaten's cult

Settlement is an order

Oodgeroo's editor made her Bora Ring
(The shape of her Bora Ring story)
A rectangle

Her Rainbow Snake a rectangle

Make of that (a rectangle snake)
What you will

Reading the Aboriginal petitions of the 1920s-30s
The letters to newspapers
(1940s, 60s)
I'm struck by the theme of friendship
The black hand offered to the white

This is the clasp on the cover
Of Robert Walker's Up Not Down Mate
(The first edition; the second portrays an Aboriginal flag
And a hand against prison bars)

Walker yelled a lot his last night

Settlement and Federation and mapping
The coastline

Feeding the young man
That escaped from gaol on his birthday
He was already wearing a crucifix

To reverse Stevens: humans are earth
(Soil stone sand and sea)
They're not walking maps
From above they are points
(Pyramid points become blobs)
Numbers of people make blobs too
And sometimes rings, snakes

Hymns are of an old, Greek order
(Relatively old)

The poems of Kevin Gilbert are not like hymns
If anything they protest the loss of hymning

At least it seems that way to me

In the 'Native Settlements' like Moore River
(Featured in the film Rabbit-Proof Fence)
Young Aboriginal students read the Bible
(Just as they do in juvenile detention now)

At times they were allowed into the bush
And learned from the elders
This apparent contradiction allowed an extension
Of control
As did trivial permissions and underfeeding

The effect of the Stolen Generations is not only
One of history, the story of Gladys Gilligan
For example
Late of Moore River Native Settlement

When I read the language of Aboriginal friends
On Facebook, I see the influence of African America
A marker that they 'own'

Just as Christianity differentiates country people
From the faithless urban 'arm'

It's not just Cook that makes this poem possible
But the Wurundjeri Council
Their office at Abbotsford Convent
A short bike ride away
From where I write this in my prism
(Seen as a rectangle from above)

Yet I remember the earthquake when
This building moved (relatively) like a snake

Singing

To understand. Realisations in the shower
Now I've sung your story I know about the
Shifts in voice – it isn't all one perspective

  Ahh Ahhh Ahhhh

A saying isn't said just because it sounds good
It's broad-humoured, yet can be said plain in
Front of children. If you sing it even better

  Ahhhh Ahhh Ahh

You know one thing about a song from
The radio. You know something else when
It's coming from your own throat – that's
The note. A song doesn't belong on a page
A song isn't on it like paint. A song, a
Page make structure, make place, thing. A
Thing that can do and change and be ruined
You know that door doesn't belong to a woman
Or a man, it's rather everything you're leaving
Everything you're running to. But you sing it
Like a drowning or a jumping up through a trap
Door and it's yours. Sit down, there's a guitar
On the fire – it plays no good but it burns beaut
Ifully. Didn't you have a love like that? A life
Weren't you born here or close enough or far

Away? Didn't you drink enough wine to make
You doubt it could stand in for anything but it
Self? It was all too general, too general, too
Universal, we didn't want it, we didn't want
Anything that way, not like a novel, not like
An allegorical painting of Hope or Victory
Let that kind of suffering belong to those times
Let it all be the blinding drift of good after
Noons and nights that were just a movie of
The moon. We wanted to be – we were – shel
Tered. The song we sang then was about a dog
That had gone wild and its character was com
Plex and it saved someone's life in an unexpec
Ted way…and we didn't die: we took a good
Hard look at our lives in the words we sang
It was a joy. The song itself was the girl, the
Boy, the dance, the stimulation. It just had
Too much class to make it explicit. The song
Had moves that took us where we weren't
Supposed to go (we supposed). And we
Looked around, it was the night, the trees
And the words had changed. We ate the burnt
Guitar because we thought that's what you do

April Fools

Person 1 is ascending the lift   Person 3 is fixing a spliff on the back porch   Person 2 is lying on a bed reconsidering what they'd said to Person 1 earlier   Person 6 is eating a hamburger with the beetroot falling out as their bus arrives   Person 5 is lighting candles   Person 4 is curling salmon onto crackers   Person 2 is examining their face for acne   Persons 7 and 8 bump into each other under the wisteria   Person 2 puts their hand between Person 3's legs   Person 9 is watching *Law and Order SVU*   Person 4 watches Persons 3 and 2 and pours a drink   Person 1 remarks that Persons 7 and 8 have matching flowers in their hair   Person 5 looks goes down to the street to see if Person 9 is arriving   Person 6 is arriving with a rather dramatic stain on their chest   'I've only got two hands'   There's a large frozen lump on the bench   'Ugh did you clean your teeth with Shiraz'

Person 8 is looking for a glass and finds one that seems clean, but then notices it's lipsticked   Person 2 looks and sounds dopey   Person 1 smiles at Person 3 with their mouth only   Person 6 takes off the Kristin Hersh CD   Person 10 hands Person 2 a gift: handpainted rubber bands   Person 5 fiddles with the air conditioning   Person 9 looks up to the apartment and sees three bats – what could it mean but luck? The maidenhair's wilting, like it's sweetpeas   'Everything's been washed'   Person 6...   Person...   'That's the railroad, or still is'

Person 8 controls the vinyl 'What are the best and worst books on this shelf, in your opinion?' Person 5 shows Person 4 a magazine

'What's the shape of your life then?' 'A university waiter' 'What kind of dog's that?' 'You're very quiet' 'Person 4 made the dips', with some irony In the two main party rooms, the positions of Persons 2 and 3 and Persons 7 and 8 parallel (that is, from Person 9's point of view) 'Hah-hah-hah-ha!' 'Oh yeah?' Person 1 is 'out of cigarettes' 'Adriano Celentano' 'Where did Person 1 go?' Person 2 has rolled a rubber band onto Person 3's wrist

Person 9 is helping Person 5 down the back steps Persons 4, 7, 8 and 10 are playing Canasta Person 6 is dancing and exclaiming in mime Persons 11 and 12 arrive, look around, try the dips and leave Person 13 is reading Bolaño in a corner trying to be in light and shadow at once A vase sports the remainder of the rubber bands Persons 6 and 10 have a texta fight

Person 4 puts some of the food away Person 2 takes the pork out of the oven 'Leave them alone' Person 9 drops an icecube on the floor and apologises to it Person 5 comes in the front door and smells the pork. Gagging, they reach for the kettle Person 3 falls off the couch Persons 7 and 8 are tied together with shoelaces Person 2 places an icecube on Person 3's ear Person 4 removes it Person 1 returns, 'like a phoenix' says Person 2 in an arguably loving tone 'Is there cake?' Person 3's awake

The Clockroach

...being by the sea. There under pergolas, persimmon trees, I – we – had the time. Like raw sexy youths, prone to alternative proofs of the human kind. The soft from washing shirt, the mountainous coal in my eyes...you love and defend me. I'm taken by your voice, as wide as a three lane highway with less pollution, and country cassettes instead of roadkill. There's snow on my head: a kind of fame, the cows came home and died of natural causes, while I interpreted alien signals in the salt-white sky. There were places to go that don't exist in the West. And you are with someone else now, recovering your savoir-faire. Your rapprochement. It was civilised, and not about abrasion or boys or race effects. There was the northern rain to contend with, and my young friend, who was only too happy to learn your name, saying it over and over. There I was by the river. The gentle mockery of the beautiful teacher; the easygoing Labor voter; all the other kinds, getting up early. Won't you have more sympathy, or a lot less? Standing by the theatre like people who've just met and noticing the bad behaviour through the glass. Unable to take offense: postbox or saintly. He would talk on, as if type was going on without him, but she could only think of how rude and wrong he was and pour her cocktail in the sink. The other guy was there, with his surfboard tucked under his right eye, and the one who thought my driving dangerous enough to warrant special laws against it. There was awkwardness about beds and money; there usually is when reviews are involved. I was white with cinema, and my spider kept interrupting having children. French-themed occasions make for new kinds of relations. He sat down in the beerhouse; I said something helloish. I didn't want to go on repeating myself, doing different things every day, like a pinup banging on a dunny door. And every fit of anger brought me someone new. They were so drunk they liked it, dancing. We both liked the sunshine, and I had a different kind of Celtic charm. Sometimes you just want ease, cream and strawberries, and a chance to tell your cranky nonsense to a high-paying crowd. Well, she was a good stick with a homemade rubber band around her wrist to remind her of more comradely times. Sleep. Don't wake up. If your butt's in the air, it's the right time of year. Living here with my family, finding that a pearl is a pearl, and that all kinds of body parts can talk. I'm going to keep the rest in. But remember those meetings near the hot sun, and the icecream before the long drive home? We thought you did it just to get sick, but the phone calls said otherwise. Let's walk out into the park, where the game is to sing a union song till a wicket falls, and reality deals you a swifty; have I forgotten to leave anything? There was help and ignorance in equal measure, she liked a bit of stewed quince, and I liked her, but I needed another, and we watched the sparrows from the van. Goodness warred with anger, and I just knew the future was on the other end of the line. Losing a hand in his hair, or his cool in an email, that's where the static went. A bus: a Chinese restaurant: a piece of scorn on toast. The mooniversity shining on the handshake exam. The house was not burning, the class were just about to get into their rhythm. You like me, you want me to be here in the piazza. There's no circle, only a book. When you're ready to love, the pool will dry up. Edible berries and locusts enough for a lifetime all around. Draw them. Sing them. Change them. Hold them. The goal was now to stop changing. To have more of yesterday's cells every day. *In this poorly researched life*. The bed had feelings that weren't mine. I wore a blue tshirt for a while, pretending I was in Sydney, and wondered at the lack of appreciation. I would turn around, while the bad writer compared living to dying: death was like Reader's Digest, wasn't it? I took a few details of the older man's life, his disparagement of the annuity poets…'Wine makes them unfriendly.' The sky has words to greet me, ladidah. There's a fine art to putting it down unbalanced. Would you, the local Falstaff, tell me otherwise, of other wives you'd liked but had to now know less? At the party, the scary person and future friend, so generous. I exploited my religious apostasy for her favour, her humour, her mockery of porridge. The mildness overcame me, though it was admittedly major. He had taught me / I taught myself…a kind of script…a kind of…groundfloor html. My accent began to intrigue people, my more street tshirts (of a later decade), my thinking about…

The Picnic Waiter

There were seeds missing from the watermelon
we complain plain plain plained. Did you count them
There were seventy-five. How do you pronounce
croissant? Bridge of sighs, bridge of sighs. The job

...evolutionist is to help everyone
evolve. Adroit if nothing else, Roderick
the picnic waiter, stepped among...

reclining nongs, dweebs and spongers. A splash

...virtue there, a bolstering slice. It wasn't

... phone manner but phone illness. The idea
had come upon Roderick in Gelden's private
cinema while he held the old man's head
in his lap. Then the cameo on...

tram. The water would be warm enough in

...couple more weeks. A fried potato...

dry leek. The food comes from or goes to

...lap. Why read Romantic poetry (Long
live seduction!) to someone who's already
in your bed? Drivel is far preferable

opined Roderick silently: his hero
John Gielgud. Cabbage was a divider
he'd noticed. Coleslaw was more popular
than cooked; its popularity directly
related to the percentage of dressing
in the serve. Today it was swimming. What
colour are lemons? What colour's lemon
skin? Lemon skin handbag; lemon fur coat
Someone was drunk (deranged?) enough to draw
hopscotch squares with dark chocolate. Roderick was
urged to desist from walking in them, or
to have the decency to hop through them
Carrying a flambé goose or banana
with a sparkler: he didn't think...

insurance covered such mishaps. He
remembered – or was it a dream – falling
down steps carrying twenty cherry sundaes

...dislocating his elbow? The nurse combed
cream from his mo; his chef's hat ruined...

Look how much dressing you have: the waiter
must like you. We ready ourselves for...

pip-spitting war. The loo has a queue as
long as your once-doggy, now fishy face
There were once some fish. Single or married
Married, of course. Those that passed out had coffee

beans inserted in their nostrils. This might've
amused Roderick, had he a brace of mice
trained to scratch them out, dragging the victims'
single origin souls behind them. Instead
he placed a fan by the grater. It blew
a fine Parmesan dust over the sleepers

A Romantic Woman

Has sewn a bauble on her dress tonight
She thinks about the relation between
natural and artificial light as
she drives through the evening in a taxi
Doubt becomes her. If she were Catholic she
assumes she would've toyed with bishops...

agnostic it's jackaroos that keep her
reading colonial fiction. Danielle
loves being twenty-nine (the pathos of
it) and dreams of an earlier name like
Muriel or Jean. She smooths the violet
sash her mother would say meant 'die single
The country can be harsh like that. Next year
she might become a novelist, but for
now she's happy with the magazine world
the hair and makeup boys, donuts on Fridays
She met someone online recently who
carves his own chess pieces and has a sandy
fringe, and she'll meet Liam in the flesh tonight
Warm and soft, she says to herself warm...

soft. The night is floating with stuff: maybe
organic, but she thinks wearing a veil's
underrated. I can't wear a taxi
everywhere, she jokes to the driver who
doesn't understand why not. Danielle thinks...

her friends, their brutal ways with men and how
successful such ways are. Men are afraid
she isn't strong: yet she's been known to eat
tuna from a can (to the right music
They don't know what it takes to be her! She
wouldn't be an editor for long…

Magazines were arcades for Danielle, not
stylish training manuals. Cigarettes
or insanity she would quip (before
she quit). Her therapist said she had…

Cinderella complex but Danielle – in
a rare fiery moment – retorted…

you have complexomania! Whereas
she was a deer of the forest…

Harriet Shelley without the river
bit, or the kids. Really, her mind was drifting
into inanity. The Melbourne traffic
wasn't like a forest; she could surely
find better role models if she needed
them. She would never make anything happen
Danielle imagined Liam was probably
one of those soft, toilet-paper roll kinds…

guys with razor blades attached to the last
sheet. They love you until then. I have…

date with a bottle of gin, she thought…

a man on the side: a moment to cherish
cherish, cherish. She noticed that the clasp
on her handbag resembled a creature
with an unusual nose. She began
to conceive of a feature…

underrated beauty. She sat in the taxi
outside the foam party, the metre running
scribbling in her notebook while the humming
driver played a samba on the steering-wheel

The Grandfather

Wasn't technically a grandfather, but
a father of three: a man in his...
forties, another in his twenties...
a young boy of four, to three different...
women. He was called Grandfather within
the family though, despite neither of his
adult sons having children of their own

In his late sixties, he felt a strong sense
of well-being and love which he expressed
to his current partner Ada and their
child, called Neftalí, the birth name of...
Pablo Neruda. 'I'd give you...
anything,' he said to Neftalí...
kissing him loudly and wetly on...
side of his head, in the mildly...
discomfited and ironic...
presences of his other sons

'Anything, Grandfather?'
'Yes – why not?'
'Then
I'd like your name.' So the elderly man
and the young boy swapped names: the father...
became known as Neftalí, and the boy
as Grandfather. He's the one, thought...

Neftalí, he will be…
gratifying son. Imagine, what an
effect he will have on people, at least
while he's young, when he introduces…
himself as Grandfather! He will be big
in one way or another. A boy called
Grandfather is at least bound to have…
children. Grandfather's personality
became stern and tyrannical: nothing
like the lighthearted and loving…
example of Neftalí; Grandfather
had no experience of actual
grandfathers. Finlay, the eldest son, was
reminded of a portrayal of…
Napoleon in a movie that had
been on SBS recently. No, I
think it's Morgan Freeman, said Leif, son…
number two. 'Tonight we are going to
the orchestra', announced Grandfather…

Everyone had noticed the expansion
of Grandfather's culture…
vocabulary. He rarely said…
anything that didn't contain…
multisyllabic word. He liked a rusk
in whiskey in the evening. It was…
sudden end to parenting for Ada
who now spent more time in her studio

Grandfather would regularly read...
Neftalí's favourite story...
Nodding Of The Blue Giraffe', to him...
commissioned several paintings on this theme
from Ada. His brothers, who had...
previously shown him no more than warm
resentment, began to dote on...
respect him. They realised how bored they
had become with the previous regime

Their mothers, too, began to spend more time
at the family home, playing with...
Neftalí and reminiscing with...
Grandfather about the good old days, which
he seemed to know uncannily well. All
in all, an impressive coup. Yet though...
Grandfather maintained a stony...
imperturbability in public
in bed he worried about the business
government policy...
activities of the Greens. It all boiled
down to one thing: what kind of future was
he providing for Neftalí? He spent
many hours reading the lies in *The Age*
and on Wikipedia, trying to
keep abreast. One night, in despair...
Grandfather fell to reading Neftalí's
volumes of Marx. By morning he had...
resolved to write an essay on...

Aesthetics of Irony': 'Irony
should show traces of pain; it must be...
experiential'. Grandfather worried
about his legacy. He heard...
Gloria, Ada's Golden Labrador
yelp, and going out to the backyard...
swiftly made the transaction that he had
made only days earlier with...
Neftalí. Gloria exulted...
'Deo!', he loved his new name. Grandfather
got out of her basket and called to...
blue butterflies, 'I'm Grandfather now, so
watch your steps'. They leapt over the fence